INSTRUCTIONS FOR ARMOURERS

from 1897

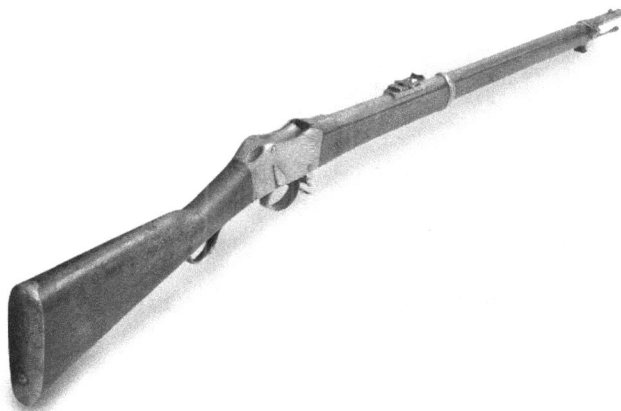

Martini-Henry

INSTRUCTIONS FOR ARMOURERS

Martini-Henry

by Frederic Faust

ISBN - 978-0-934523-55-4
editor@middle-coast-publishing.com

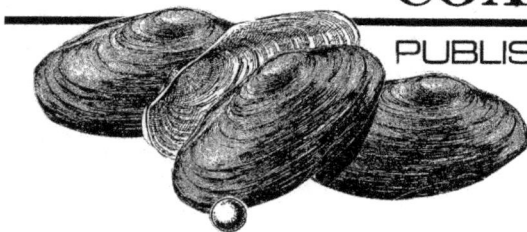

MIDDLE COAST PUBLISHING

"Good Books Are Where We Follow Our Dreams."

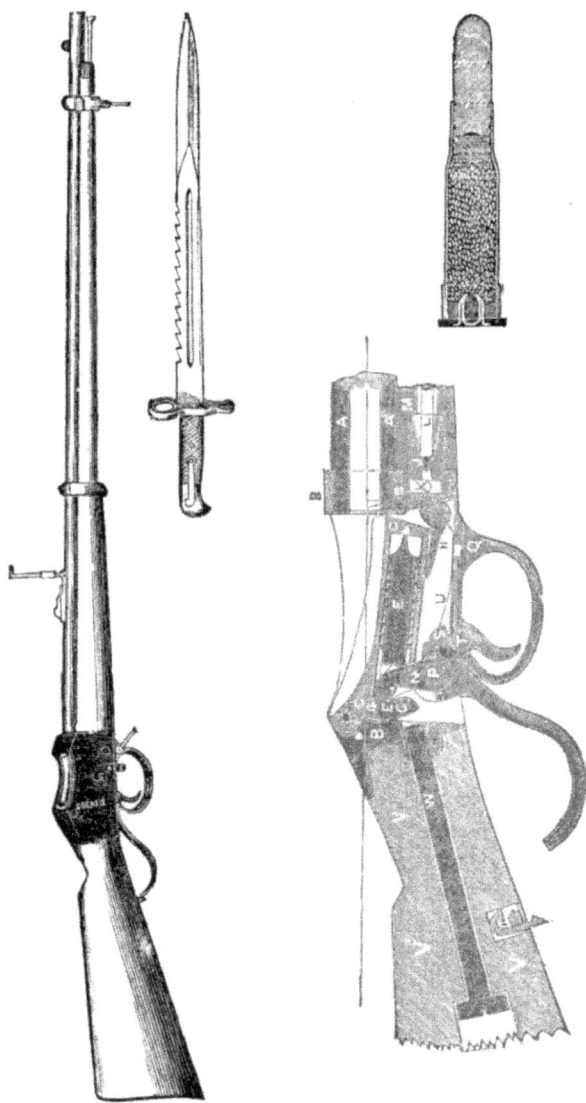

Fig. 105.—The Martini Breech loader.

.402 ENFIELD-MARTINI CONVERTED TO MARTINI-HENRY Mk IV

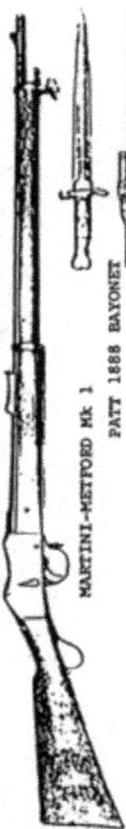

MARTINI-METFORD Mk 1

PATT 1888 BAYONET

MARTINI-ENFIELD Mk 1

MUZZLE/SIGHT COVER

Dedicated to:

Henry O. Peabody

Frederich von Martini

Alexander Henry

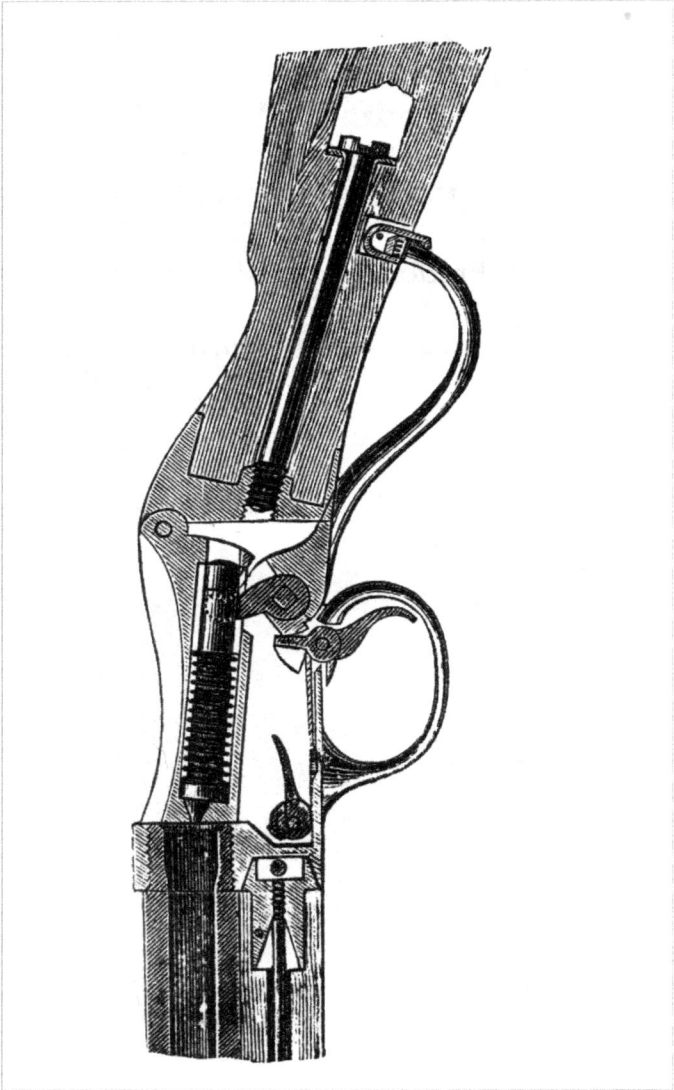

Table of Contents

1

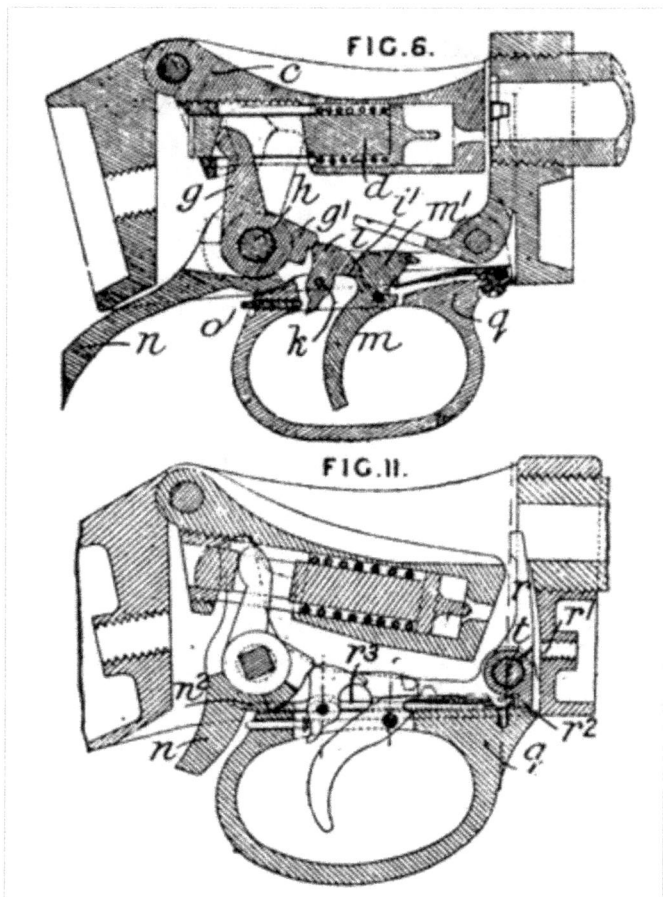

FIG. 6.

FIG. 11.

2

INSTRUCTIONS FOR THE CARE AND REPAIR OF THE MARTINI-HENRY

Keep all parts connected with the breech action perfectly clean. Use Rangoon oil only for this purpose. Cutting substances, such as emery, sand-paper, et cetera, or of the buff stick is strictly forbidden.

Editor's note: Rangoon oil was a British colonial cleaning agent and a rust preventative, a tenacious oil boasting a slow evaporation rate. It kept firearms free of rust in hot, steamy jungle conditions.

When cleaning take care to not injure the face of the block, especially the striker hole. Do not enlarge the chamber by cleaning. Only wire gauze or an oiled rag should be used for this purpose. A bright chamber should not to be insisted upon. See instructions for cleaning magazine arms. Occasionally apply Rangoon oil to the following parts of the action

- ✔ Knuckle and knuckle seat of the block.
- ✔ Axis pin of the block.
- ✔ Lever ends and seat in the block.
- ✔ Lever and tumbler axis.
- ✔ Trigger axis.

- ✔ Trigger nose and spring.
- ✔ Extractor axis
- ✔ Main spring and striker
- ✔ Stop nut and tumbler.

DIRECTIONS FOR STRIPPING THE ACTION

Close the action.

First remove any dirt in the slit in the block axis pin, then knock it out the pin with a drift.

Depress the lever and hold down the front end of the block with the left thumb. Close the lever, and the block will spring out.

Take out the block. Rotate the keeper screw until its curve lies fair with the curve in the stop nut's head.

Unscrew the stop nut. The striker and main spring will then fall out.

Turn the keeper screw head of the lever axis fair with the axis hole. Press out the axis pin.

Take out the tumbler.

Turn out the extractor axis screw, and remove the extractor, trigger guard, and lever.

Rotate the screw holding the trigger spring counterclockwise. Remove the spring.

Turn out the triggers' axis screw. Take out the trigger.

DIRECTIONS FOR STRIPPING
FURNITURE, BARREL AND STOCK RIFLE
M-E MARK I

Draw the clearing rod by first unscrewing the
rod counter-clockwise until the rod draws
straight out.
Remove the upper band pin.

Partly un-turn band screws and take off bands.
do not remove the lower band's stop pin.

Pull off stock.

Take off the butt plate.

Turn out the stock bolt, and remove the butt
stock.

CARBINES ARTILLERY M-M MARK II and MARK III, M-E MARK I

Draw the cleaning rod by first unscrewing the rod in a counterclockwise direction.
Remove the nose cap screw, drive the nose cap off the fore-end, and rotate it so the fore-sight passes through the slot in the nose cap.

Remove the barrel's stud pin. At the breech end, use a wood drift, to drive the stock fore-end off the barrel stud

Pull off stock from the barrel's muzzle so that the hook disengages from the end of the body..

As directed for the rifles

For M.-E, Mark I rifle, see (4) for carbines.

DIRECTIONS FOR ASSEMBLING ACTION, BARREL, STOCK, AND FURNITURE. RIFLE M-E MARK I

Replace the butt stock. Be sure to position the stock bolt washer in its proper place within the stock butt.

Tighten the stock bolt.

Screw the butt plate onto the stock.

Place the hook fore-end in place. Replace the bands.

Turn home the band screws in a clockwise direction.

Replace the upper band pin.

Replace the clearing rod in its groove

Place the trigger in the trigger guard

Tighten the axis screw

Replace the trigger spring, taking care that the nose of the trigger spring is under the trigger.

Screw in the trigger spring screw.

Place the lever and tumbler in the trigger guard. Slide it along with the lever and tumbler into the body.

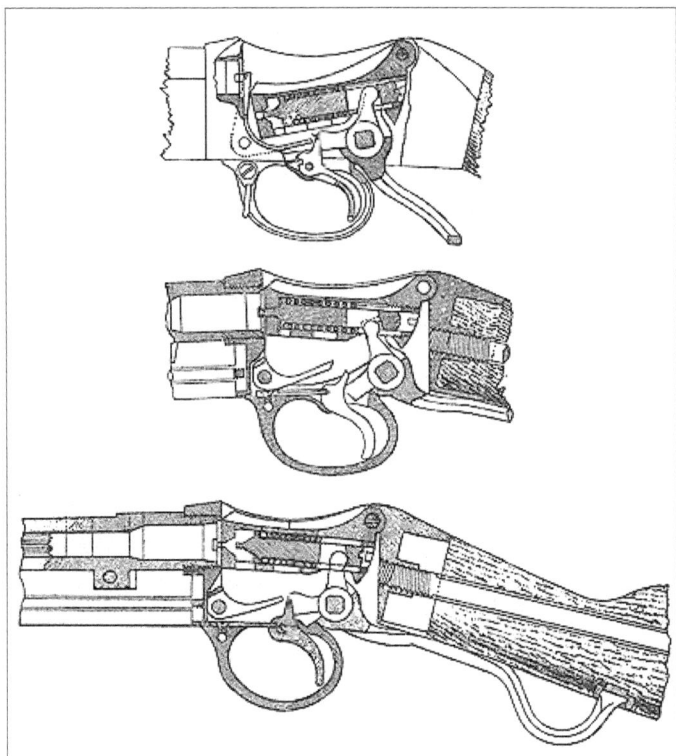

Replace the axis pin, so its indicator points upwards towards the direction of the block axis pin.

Screw down the round keeper screw head into its proper bedding

Replace the extractor and draw down the axis screws main spring

9

Screw home the stop nut

Turn the keeper screw head into its bedding.

Rotate the striker until the broadest side of the slot faces downwards.

Place the block in the body with the front end lowest.

While holding the lever with the right hand, press the indicator forward with the tumbler, the trigger being pushed back by the forefinger.

With the heel of the left hand, press hard on the knuckle of the block force it into its seat.

Simultaneously depress and work the striker into the block. Drop in the lever and work the lever to position the tumbler in the slot in the striker.

Compress the split sides of the block axis pin to place.

Insert it into the body.

† *For M.-E., Mark I rifle, see (3) for carbines.*

CARBINES (ARTILLERY)

1 & 2 As directed for the rifle.

Place the hook fore-end in the body thereby engaging within the recess, then press the stock up to the barrel at the muzzle.

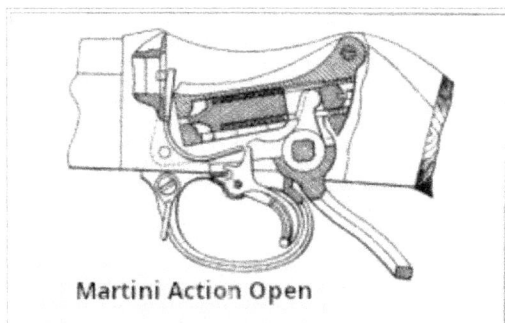

Martini Action Open

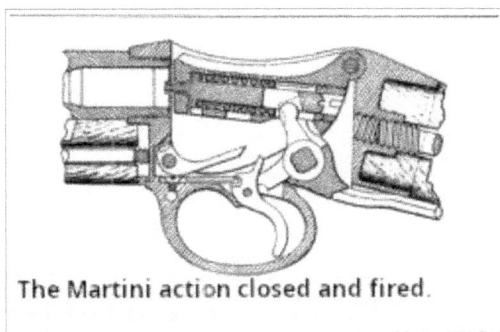

The Martini action closed and fired.

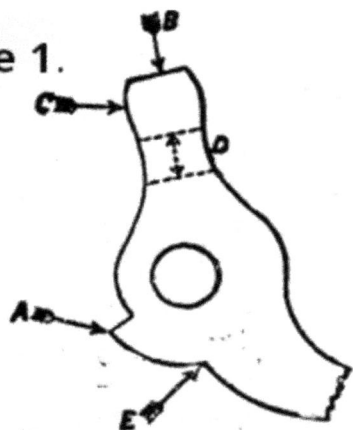

Figure 1.

REPLACING COMPONENTS. RIFLES AND CARBINES

Adjustment in Loading Position

If the block stands too tall, then the bearing surface at A **(Figure 1)** should be lowered. Depress the lever by striking it with a punch to the breadth of the mating surface on the tumbler. If removing more than '01 of an inch is required, then simply fit a new lever.

With the block in its firing position, if the striker impacts the cap too high, know that removing an amount metal can bring it in line. Removing no more than .01 of an inch from the lever horn's bearing surface of at B will rectify the error.

In the alternative, should the striker strike the cap too low, draw out horns of the lever between the lines indicated at D not to exceed .01 of an inch. In doing so, take care not to spread the horns at C.

Should the block lay too low, add material not exceeding .01 of an inch. Carefully draw out the metal bearing surface at A. No more than .01 of an inch be required. If so, fit a new lever.

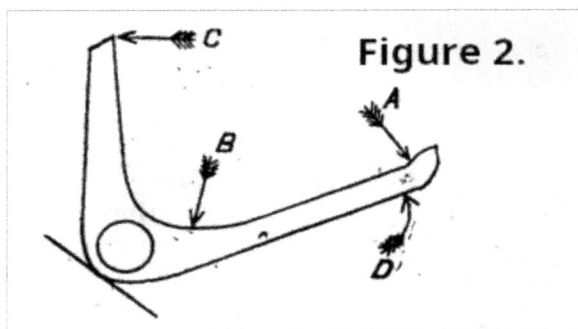

Figure 2.

Extractor.— Extractor.— With the block at it loading position, point A (**Figure 2)** should be just free from the underside of the block.

With the block depressed to its lowest position, it bears on point B, holding the extractor firm. Should the lever touch the guard preventing the block from doing that (E), file the guard to allow the lever to clear. Point D on the guard should be (when the extractor is at its lowest position. If it does not bed down, look for the fault on the head of the trigger spring screw. If this stands too proud, flatten it with a file.

Trigger.-- In replacing a trigger, the nose must not be "touched in" when making the pull-off. Adjust by altering the angle of the tumbler bent by scraping the face.

Trigger spring.— When replacing a trigger spring, the head of the screw must bed well down on the spring. And that the point should not bear down on the guard swivel screw.

Guard.— In replacing the guard, place it in the body with the indicator fixed in position. Note how the guard will drop freely into the body without side pressure. If the extractor axis hole does not fit fair in both the body and the guard and body file, the nib resting on the front of the body. If required, run a tap to regulate the hole and insert the axis screw: Ensure the indicator revolves freely.

Tumbler.-- When replacing a tumbler, it should-pass firmly onto, but not need to be driven, hard upon the squares of the indicator. It should work freely between the horns of the lever.

Indicator.—Remarks same as upon tumbler.

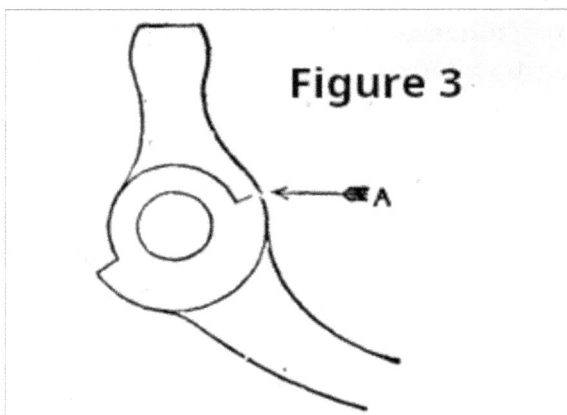

Figure 3

Lever.-- When replacing a lever, when the lever is depressed, the bearings at point A **(Figure 3)** should be free. Otherwise, it prevents the block from taking its complete fall. The end of the lever must drop freely into its catching block. Care must also be taken so that the lever firmly beds on its seat on the underside of the socket end of the body.

Levers issued with spare parts are intended for long buttstocks. So naturally, it follows short butts require setting in. A slight blow with a mallet is necessary to make them drop freely into the lever catch block. Levers for long butts are issued in preference to levers for short butts because the adjustment required by the former to fit them to short butts is simpler than adjusting a lever for a short butt to a long butt.

Striker.—When replacing, take care so that the significant part of the slot is downwards and that the striker is correct to gauge for length and radius of the point.

Examination of Strikers.—Use the .064-in. Gauge cartridge dummy with its empty primer hole filled with soap level with the base disc. To test the condition of the point of the striker. Load the rifle with the gauge cartridge dummy and fire.

On withdrawing the dummy, an impression of the striker's point will be found in the soap. At least, it will if the striker is perfect. Should the striker fail to make an impression in the soap when the rifle is fired, the striker's point is likely broken.

Stock. —To replace the stock butt, first, remove the butt plate. Unscrew the stock bolt and remove the washer. Should the new stock not draw firmly home when the bolt is screwed up, then add a second washer. Should the tip of the stock bolt protrude beyond the body, it interferes with the range of motion of the block when extracting. To remedy additional washers may be stacked up inside the stock.

In replacing the rifle's fore-end, M.-E., Mark I, and carbines, A.C.M-M., Mark III, and M.-E., Mark I, care must be taken that the stock does not spring from the muzzle but drops fair home, or it will affect the shooting of the barrel.

Easing springs. — Open the action. Place your thumb on the thumb seat and your forefinger on the trigger. Curl your remaining fingers under the guard. Without touching the lever, press the trigger firmly. Close the lever. Clasp the bow of the lever and the small of the butt with the right hand. Secure the lever in its catch. Nota Bene

"Never ease springs when a cartridge is chambered."

How to adjust pull-off.— Assemble the guard with a block assembly, lever, and tumbler. Regulate the pull-off by the bent, from 2 to 2½ lb., without the trigger spring. Insert the trigger spring. If too heavy bring the pull-off to the

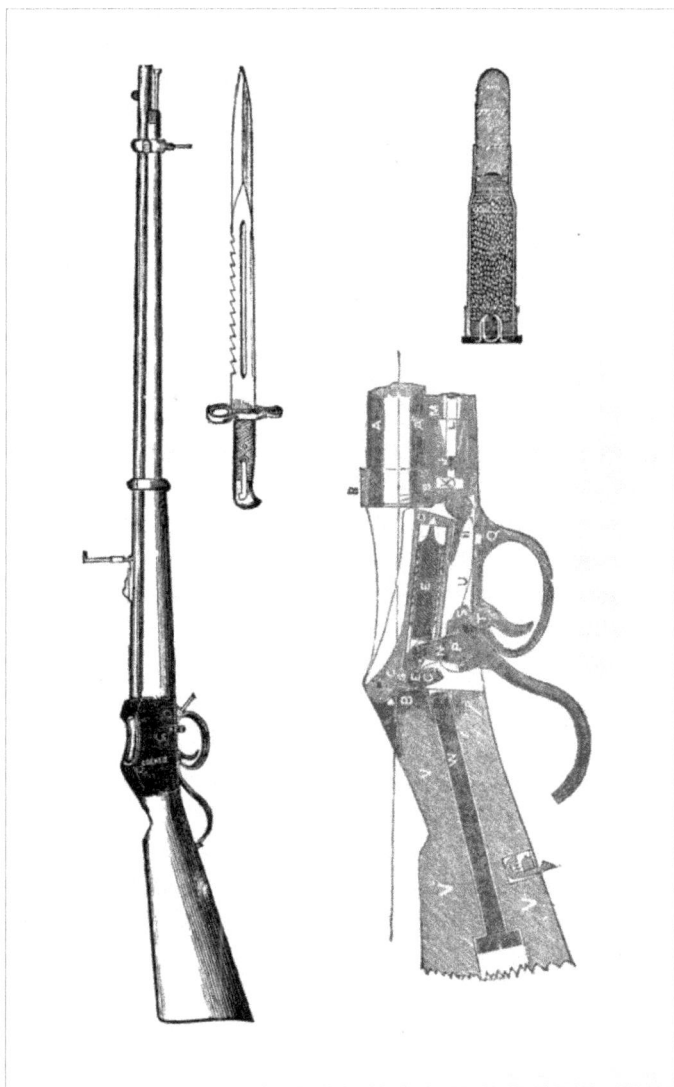

regulation weight of 6- to 8-pounds by filing the underside of the spring. Or, in the alternative, put in a stronger spring. If too light, ensure the spring is screwed firmly down by the screw. In replacing a trigger spring, the "pull-off" adjust as described above.

Gauge, action.— The "gauge, action" is issued to armourer-serjeants and others solely to test a component, or components, of any rifle which appears to be defective. For this purpose, the parts of the rifle's action may be assembled in the "gauge, action" when the working can be seen and any defective parts noticed.

Should there be any doubt as to which component is at fault, the issue can be set to rest by removing and replacing it. Substitute the suspected part that corresponds to one from the "gauge, action," which, being of correct form, should work well if the other components are in good order.

Spare parts.—When installing a spare part bearing a date of manufacture in a rifle or carbine, the spare part's date is to be placed by the armourer near the S, found on the self-same spare part. If the lever fails to close on pulling the trigger, indicating the action is not in good order, and the lever must be pressed home by the right hand.

THE MARTINI-HENRY RIFLE.

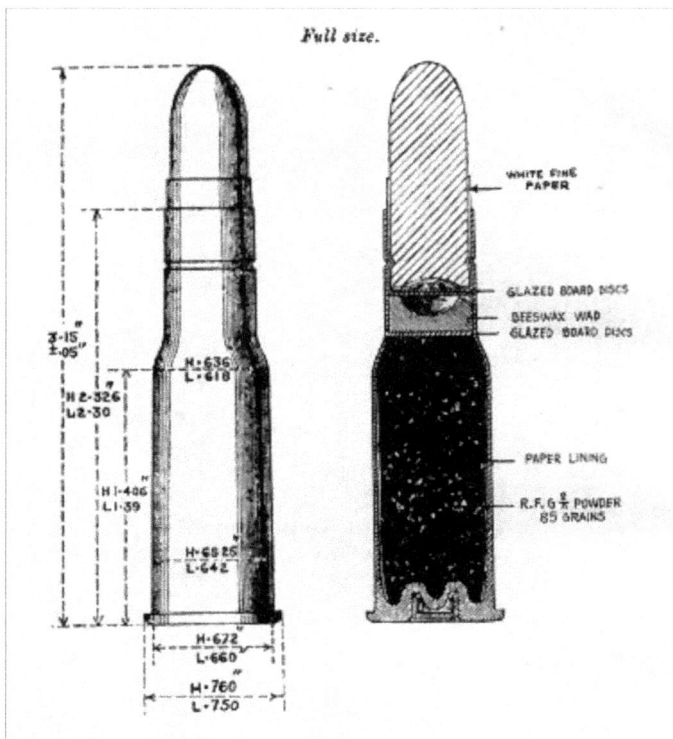

Full size.

WHITE FINE
PAPER

GLAZED BOARD DISCS

BEESWAX WAD

GLAZED BOARD DISCS

PAPER LINING

R.F. G² POWDER
85 GRAINS

3·15"
2·05"

H 2·326
L 2·30

H 1·406
L 1·39

H·636
L·618

H·68 25
L·642

H·672
L·660

H·760
L·750

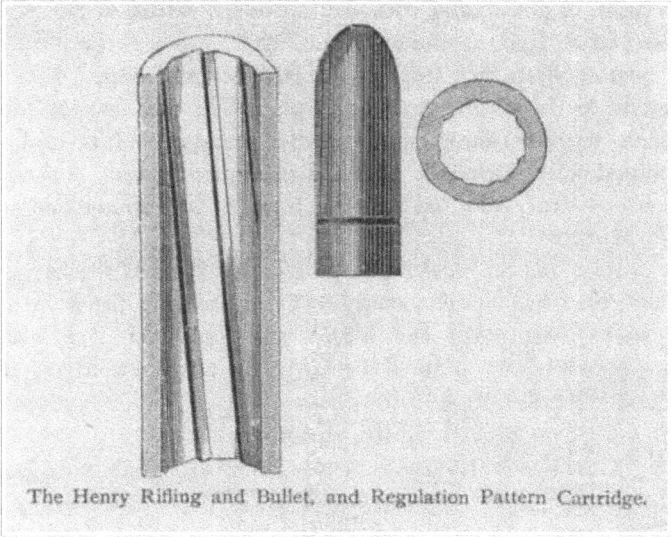

The Henry Rifling and Bullet, and Regulation Pattern Cartridge.

A cross-section of Henry rifling and its bullet

№ 1. Carbine, 450 bore.

Solid Bullet. 380 grs.
Powder. 55 grs.

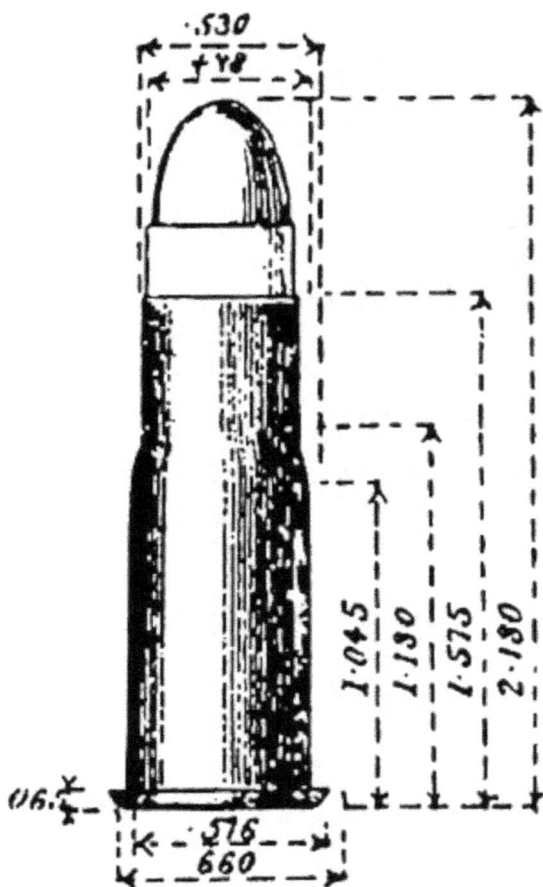

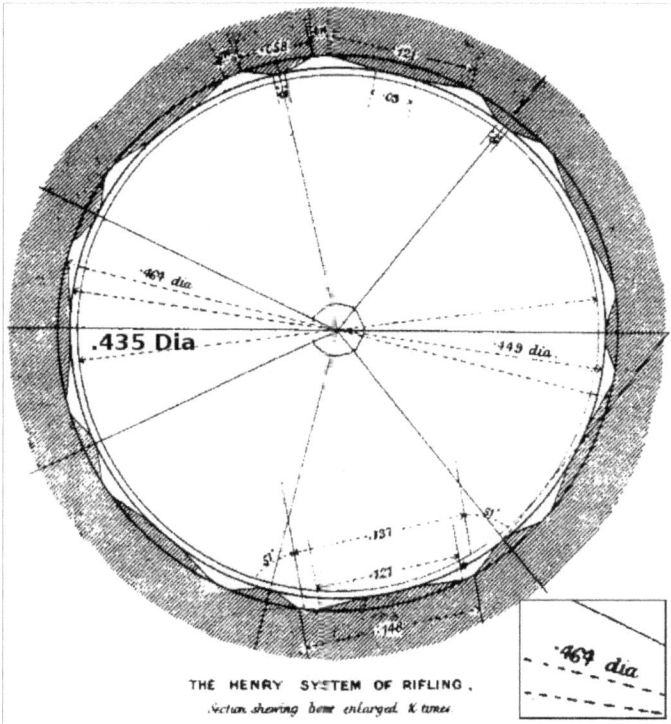

.469 dia

.435 Dia

.449 dia

.058

.121

.65

.137

.127

.146

9°

9°

9°

.469 dia

THE HENRY SYSTEM OF RIFLING.
Section showing bore enlarged X times

25

Henry's Rifling — Longitudinal section.

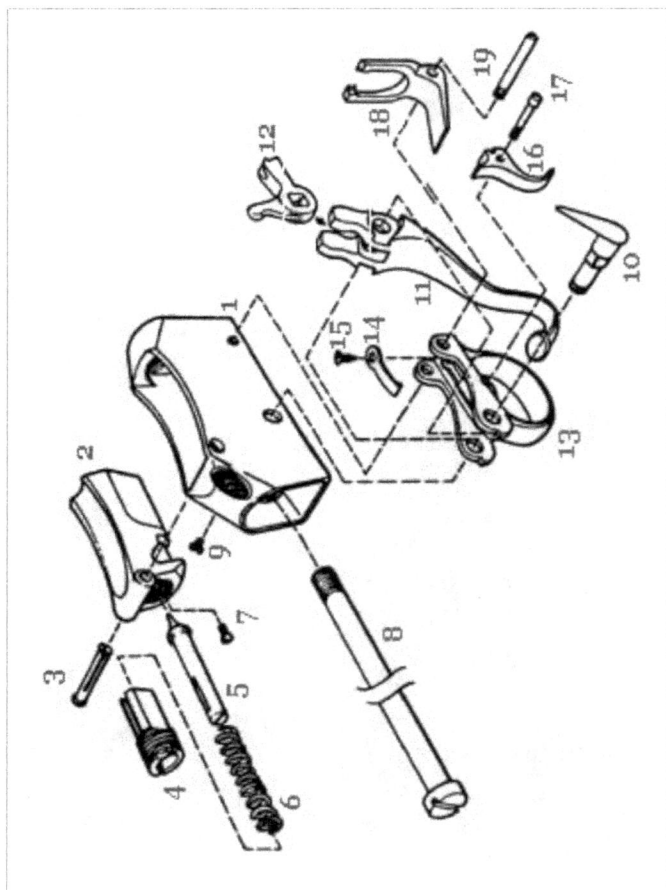

www.ingramcontent.com/pod-product-compliance
Lightning Source LLC
Chambersburg PA
CBHW060647030426
42337CB00018B/3496